52 Leadership Tips

How to Lead Through Inspiration
- NOT Intimidation

Jean A. Sturgill

Realizing Your Winning Potential
ISBN: 978-1-943620-01-2

Dedicated to
Jesus Christ

Contents

Consider Your Style of Leadership

Common Styles

Two of the popular styles of leading include authoritative, and leading by fear. Neither are the most effective. To make my point, consider how these play out when leading a team of volunteers. They will not be bossed, and they will not be intimidated. (If your current leadership style is to either lead by authority or to lead by fear, consider taking a position in a volunteer organization. It's the best place to practice leading in a more effective way.)

Other styles of leading include leading by committee and what I call guided self-direction which can also be guided group-direction.

When leading by committee, the committee will usually still be guided, and the response to actions and decisions come back on the committee. Since the committee is acting, individuals have some insulation from repercussions.

Leaders, Influencers, and the Person in Charge

The person in charge – in committee or otherwise – may or may not be the most influential, and they may not be the real leader. The influential person will often be the person who has the most experience, knowledge, or particular skills / talents needed in the situation. The leader will be the person who can rally the most support for an idea. The person in charge is the person at the top who assumes responsibility for the outcome.

When You Are in Charge and Want to Lead

The best leadership style, and the one that takes the most thought, is guided group- / self- direction. We'll call it guided direction for short. For the purpose of our *52 Leadership Tips*, we will assume that you're the person in charge over a team. It is your job to lead the team and have the most influence.

While you are gaining influence, if there is a more experienced person, you may wish to agree or defer to that person's suggestions if you trust they have the best suggestions. To go against the best suggestions, would only erode your credibility. You may also wish to confer privately with this person before holding any group meetings. Always give this person credit for ideas, but the private meeting will give you a chance to reflect first.

Guided direction is done by leading the group to identify and agree on goals through a question and answer session. This requires you to have put in the necessary research and thought and to have formed your tentative decision before you start. Statistics can be brought in to firm up the need to make a choice and to influence or guide the direction of the conversation. In addition, the use of facts (stats, demographics, and studies) adds to your credibility and the ability to see and influence the needed direction.

Summary

If done correctly, guided direction will set you up for a successful meeting with a predetermined outcome. The best decisions will then be the most obvious, and everyone will be on the same page. I like to call that "getting all the fishies to swim in the same direction."

Happy Leading!
Jean

Addressing the Fearful Team

Did you know that when you assume a leadership position, you typically inherit the reputation of the leadership style of leaders who went before you in the lives of each of the members of the team? In short, newly placed leaders are often viewed by whatever stereotype exists in the minds of the team members.

If the leaders who came before you lead by fear, you may inherit a fearful team, and a fearful team can be a challenge.

Before you can implement change – to bring them to the guided self-directed style that I explained in Tip #1, you must know if your team is fearful. You need to understand what they are thinking, and how that affects performance.

The Fearful Team

Characteristics of a fearful team:

- Reluctant to try new things
- Resists giving input
- Has become less creative / innovation stifled

- Exhibits more stress than expected
- Has a larger than expected turnover rate
- Has an atmosphere of secrecy / mutiny

Fear tends to lead to folks feeling unappreciated, and they act accordingly. They are simply marking time to the end of the day, the next job, or retirement. They won't go beyond what they view is safe, and they won't go the extra step to improve processes where they do not directly receive a benefit. The goal is to get by. Pride in work is gone. Excitement has waned. Happiness is gone.

A team that is fearful is also a team that is faithless. They do not have faith that they will continue to have a job. They do not have faith in you. You may be seen as the enemy to the status quo in which they have become accustomed, and you are the taskmaster to be feared.

If you are having trouble connecting to your team, this may be the reason for your troubles.

Also note, innovation requires folks take pride in their work and take the initiative to move the company forward when they see the opportunity. Hence, fear is counterproductive and has to be addressed / challenged.

The Road to Change

If you can get folks to participate, having discussions as mentioned in Tip #1 will help draw them out. Your encouraging response will elicit more participation.

If that doesn't work, suggestion boxes, contests, and bonuses (even small things like having pizza brought in) can all create excitement. If they are done frequently and used to draw out and reward / acknowledge good ideas and good work, they can be relationship and expectation changing.

Summary

You will need to create new experiences and expectations for your team. Your team needs to feel appreciated, and they will need to see that you are open to their ideas. Let them see that you want to have a warm, fuzzy, friendly work environment where they can look forward to spending their day. Encourage innovation.

Happy Leading!
Jean

The Character of a Real Leader

In 2006, I found myself in a situation where I needed to make a decision – or perhaps it would be more accurately described as a series of decisions. At the heart of this challenge was the need of an accurate twelve-month forecast. Without experience in this area, I could not do it. The task was too great. The information was too slim (at least in my opinion). I was stuck. Any forecast that I made would be an uneducated guess at best.

What would you do?

After much prayer, I found myself telling the person above me that I trusted him to do what was right by me, and later when the time came to make that decision, I let him do it. He had experience that I did not have, and the integrity to do what was fair and just.

What's the Value?

In my case, the decision made was the right one. The forecast was the best it could be. More than that, I knew that any decision that person made that would affect me would be fair. I never had to worry about being mistreated.

It should be obvious, but I'll be blunt. When a team cannot trust the leader in one area, it's a real faith buster in all areas. When a leader is unreliable, inconsistent, dishonest, or unethical, the team cannot function as it should apart from the leader because the leader has to be there to make the next decision. The team won't have faith in their own decisions because they don't know how to anticipate the decision that the leader would make. They also won't trust the leader to deal fairly with them.

When a leader is trustworthy – has integrity, it takes a lot of the guesswork out of decisions. The ethical "right thing" is the answer to any problem. The team will be less stressed, and make more decisions on their own. Their job will be easier, and they will be encouraged to work harder for the outcome because they know that they will be treated fairly no matter what bumps they encounter.

The Leader as Advocate

One of the most important things a leader can do is be a trustworthy advocate for the team when representing them to upper management. The first goal of the leader in this scenario is not to unfairly favor the team, but to be fair in representation of them. The second goal of the leader is to seek the best outcome for the team in the decisions (of upper management) . . . In short, they expect you not to throw them under the bus, but to seek to support and express their needs.

Summary

A leader who can be trusted is more likely to be followed. A leader who cannot be trusted will most likely have more turnover due to stress, and be suspect in the eyes of the team. He will also have more questions asked of him than necessary because the team will not feel they can make a decision without his input.

Remember, always represent your team well to upper management. While it's not your job to defend their errors, it's also not your job to unnecessarily speak ill of them. Often your spin on a situation can make it seem better or worse than it really is. Speak wisely and with character.

Happy Leading!
Jean

Now, About You – NOT

You are happily working away when someone walks by. You ask a question, and the response is to berate you. What do you do?

- Get your feelings hurt
- Get mad and show it
- Lash out
- Internalize your emotions

If you choose anything on the above list, you lose. We ALL have our weak moments, but there is a better path. You must understand what it is before you can choose it.

It Starts With You

Before you can really be your very best at leading people, you must dump the baggage. All of the responses listed above make you the focus. They are self-centered because they are about you, and most of the time, you aren't really the focus at all. If you are always assuming that what is said and done is about you, you will waste valuable time, energy, resources, hurt the feelings of others, and have hurt feelings needlessly yourself.

Having a thin skin – as the expression goes – will only harm and hold you back.

The winning response is no response – internally or externally. Ignore the berating. Yes, acknowledge that you heard the person speaking to you, but choose not to participate in bad behavior even internally. Treat it as if it did not happen.

You might be thinking, "Jean! How can I let folks off the hook so easily?" Instead, ask yourself, "Why do I keep agreeing to let other folks hold me back?"

In order to not respond and be more successful, you will really have to believe in your own self-worth. It's easier to not respond and to let go of things if you realize that what is being said isn't true just because someone else said it, and you are under no obligation to make them believe differently. Free yourself of that baggage.

If you react to every little thing that comes your way, not only will you typically look bad, but you won't get much done. Not an excuse for the person that berated you, but what if that person had been handed divorce papers that morning? What if the news had been a terminal illness? Do you think you would feel good for reacting? Do you think you would be seen as a hero in the office? No matter what your response, you lose.

Response of a Genius

Do you think Thomas Edison was successful? Do you think that he spent his time thinking about all the things folks said to him or about him? It's said that he tried over a thousand, some say 5 or 10 thousand, ways to make a light bulb. When asked about his failure, his view was that he had not failed. He had successfully discovered ways to not do it. The exact quote varies, but that is the heart of it.

He won because he focused on the task, and you can win big too!

Summary

Obviously, Edison was a very positive, determined person. We can take a lesson here. Look at your personal failures as discovering ways to not live life. Look at your business failures as ways to not accomplish your tasks or ways to not approach people.

Put your past behind you. Remember, sometimes when folks speak, they are reacting to something other than you. Be different, and don't react. When you feel attacked, stay focused on the topic and ignore the attack. Don't allow them to make it personal – and don't internalize the negative.

Happy Leading!
Jean

Are You the Clueless Leader?

Consider your local civics clubs or business organizations. You may have seen the time when two leaders in nearly identical situations got very different results. One leader (team) may have had wild success, but the other failed. I've seen it more than once.

Why? Leadership or lack thereof.

But, but, but….. Wait! Hold on! What if…..

No buts. No what ifs.

Responsibility of Leadership

Leadership is more than pointing your finger and hoping folks do what you say. You must understand the consequences of your action and lack of action. You must be able to get folks to do the work and work together. You must know where you are going and how to get there, and you must do what is necessary (legal and ethical) to make that happen. It's your responsibility.

Failure is always seen as the fault of leadership. Success is the fruit of teamwork – and credit goes to the team. No one person can make something succeed, but a leader who moves in the wrong direction (or not at all), can - with or without the assist of the team - fail. Even a leader with great ideas, will still fail when the team won't support the objectives. That's also the leader's fault.

What about the economy? Life events?

While all these things can have an effect, it still comes down to leadership. Yes, a great leader can have bad results (or even fail), but the results will typically be better than that of a poor leader.

The Measuring Stick

Figuring out if you are a good leader (have a clue) can be tricky. After all, we don't know what we don't know.

Using the bottom line as a measuring stick, compare current growth to the growth of 1) prior years, 2) the market sector, 3) your competition, and 4) your clients. Where your team is concerned, compare their attitude and turnover rate to prior years and to other teams in the organization or the organization as a whole.

This should give you a pretty good idea of how you are doing as a leader.

What If You Find Out You Don't Have a Clue? What Do You Do?

First, be sure that the folks on the team you are leading are very wise and knowledgeable about what they are doing, have proven themselves, and get good results.

Second, surround yourself with great advisors - great people who have the answers, and listen carefully to them. Then, make the best decisions you can. How do you know if you have the right people? Look at their track record. Were they successful doing what you are doing or something very similar? Have they been where you are or faced the same challenges you are facing?

Not everyone on your advisory team has to be within the company. You don't want to break any confidentialities, but in certain situations, an outside expert can be just the thing you need. Look to successful peers and field experts.

Summary

If the team fails, it's going to be seen as your fault. Find out if you are in over your head. If you don't have a clue, get a clue by getting folks on the team you are leading and on your advisory team that have the information that you need to be successful. – Kick your ego to the curb, and find these folks!

Happy Leading!
Jean

Why You
Need an Accountability Partner

Accountable for what?

Perhaps you are thinking, "I always do the right thing."
Wake up! Everyone thinks they know what the right
thing to do is, but in reality we all have those situations
where what's right can't be defined by morality or legality.
Sometimes right is defined by perspective. Sometimes it's
defined by wisdom. Some things just aren't wise.

. . . And besides all that, you'll get more accomplished, and
be a better leader with an accountability partner.

Your decisions

Let's say for example that you have a position open in your
company. You advertise, have lots of applicants, and now
you must decide which person to hire. Do you hire the
person with the most technical skills? The person with the
most people skills? Do you hire someone who will work for
less? Do you hire the person who may not have the very

best people or technical skills, but who will work for a little less and has a wife and three children to feed?

Would you play favorites in the scenario above based on cash, need, skills, or the perceived ability to get along with others?

An accountability partner may ask you thought provoking questions. Do you really need to hire anyone? What will be the impact on the current employees? Did you observe how that person relates to the other employees? Will that person move the company ahead?

Your productivity

If your accountability partner is chosen wisely, you can make great strides in productivity. Learning curves can be shortened. Errors in plans and judgment can be caught. New resources can be uncovered, and your focus on the task at hand can be sharpened. All these things can move your team ahead.

More specifically, when others have eyes and ears in the same field as you do, you can learn from them. When you share what you've learned, it reinforces it. When you have questions, you may find that the other person has fought that battle, explored that resource, or can point you in the direction of someone with an answer.

The right accountability partner can provide you with the following benefits:

- See your blind spot
- Offer alternative view points
- Offer business changing ideas
- Keep you on track with your goals
- Inspire you to do more

How often to meet?

As often as necessary, and only you can know what that is. I do better with weekly meetings, but I've found multiple partners helpful too.

As I'm writing this, I have two partners and a group. I call one partner every week. I call another about every two weeks. I meet with the group about once per month – and my weekly partner is in that group too. The weekly call keeps me thinking about what I'm doing. We are both speakers, and that focus and sharing ideas moves us ahead in that field. The bi-weekly call helps me to plan that out a little further, and – since we both write – the focus is more about writing. The monthly group, SMART, helps me think out further. (SMART – Speakers, Meeting Planners and Agents Round Table was started by Jean Robor and myself as an educational meeting. The members share ideas, and we've added time to share goals.) It challenges me to ask myself, "Can I really do that in 30 days?"

That's about 7 times a month that I'm learning from others, sharing my ideas, asking questions, and reporting on what I've accomplished.

If you choose to have multiple accountability partners, decide – as I have done – on the function of each.

Summary

Accountability partners can help you go places that you'd never think to go on your own by sharing the journey. Their experience is a benefit that you won't want to overlook. You will hopefully see a bump in productivity, a shortened decision making process (if for no other reason than you have a sounding board), and exponential growth of knowledge, resources, and confidence.

All of this will make you a better leader.

Happy Leading!
Jean

Why Do I Have to Yell to Be Heard?

Actually, while yelling always elicits a response, it doesn't always get you heard. From your perspective you think you got your point across. From your team's perspective you have just treated them badly. I've seen the following responses to leaders who yell:

- Tears
- Quitting (if not immediately, soon)
- Talking behind the leader's back to clients
- Distraction

While tears and quitting are not what you are hoping to achieve, the last two responses can really hurt your business.

Talking: I have had folks talk to me – their client – about their leader. If they'll tell me, who else are they telling? When they tell the story, it's always about how they are treated. Words like rage, temper, hotheaded, and other unflattering terms are used.

Distraction: I've witnessed entire afternoons wasted because a leader yelled and then left. The team could not work at their maximum potential because of the blowup.

Net result: loss. Whatever learning could have come from the conversation that was held – or perhaps wasn't held – was lost. The only thing remembered was that something – often unknown – upset the leader.

If you want your team to understand, remember, and respond to the correction, you don't have to be loud; you have to be articulate.

Most of the time communication fails for one of three reasons.

- The leader doesn't have the team on the same page
- The leader doesn't have the concept clear in his own head
- The leader doesn't articulate the point effectively

Information always seems clear to us when we are the one presenting it, but that really isn't always the case.

Before You Correct, Get Your Team on the Same Page

The best way to do this is take a breath and ask the team, "Why?" You need to know what they were thinking before you can address it.

When one of our boys was about three, we walked out to the backyard where we saw a robin looking for worms in a pile of leaves. Later, I asked him to put food out for the birds. I meant to put it out at the birdfeeder. Within just a few seconds, he was gone. I took off running around the house to look for him. My heart skipped a beat as I was afraid he might have gotten into the road. When I found him, he was out at the pile of leaves. I had missed seeing him because he had gone around some of our outbuildings and was out of my site. When I found him, we talked about what he had been thinking and what I meant.

Granted, this was a child, but we can all get on the wrong page. It just takes a missed word in the instructions or some missed piece of information.

Before you correct ALWAYS ask, "Why?"

Before You Correct, Get Your Point Clear in Your Head

Have you read conversations on social networks? Sometimes one person will argue a point one way, and then they argue it another. It could be that they have two points, and they have mashed the two points into one blurry point. I've been guilty of this myself.

Before you correct your team, be sure that YOU really understand what and why you are correcting them. Did they try something new, and it failed? Were they careless?

Remember, if you correct innovation, you may stifle it. Pinpoint the exact mistake that you are correcting so that the effectiveness of the correction is maximized.

Before You Correct, Be Sure You Can Articulate the Point Effectively

The previous two points go a long way toward resolving this, but timing also needs to be considered.

Addressing issues at 4:55 when folks leave at 5 won't get your point across. In many cases, they have already mentally checked out. If a long weekend is coming up, your point will be gone from their minds before they return.

Summary

Yelling doesn't have the effect you might think. Instead, articulate your points of correction effectively by having everyone on the same page, having the point clear in your head, and having good timing.

You will look better, and it will make a difference for the team!

Happy Leading!
Jean

6 Steps to Eliminating Many Mistakes

As I was standing in line at the post office, the phone rang. It was one of my best friends. I was supposed to be having breakfast with her, and I was late. I had already stood her up at least once. Now, it had slipped my mind yet again. I hurried to meet her.

I was really very upset with myself. It was not like me to do that. The only reason – not an excuse but a reason – I could figure that it happened was that I had two calendars – a personal calendar, and a business calendar. As I became busier, I would skip looking at the personal calendar because I didn't have much on it.

Obviously, that split system was a really bad idea. When I realized my issue, I corrected it. Fortunately, I had a really forgiving friend.

Here are six steps that you can take when working with a team to eliminate many of their mistakes. Of course, you can use this with your own mistakes too.

1) Consider all the reasons your team could find for why a mistake is made before you discuss it with them. This will give you time to think about potential solutions.

2) Ask the team for their reasons or what they think was the issue. You may have overlooked something. (I had two calendars.)

3) Make a plan for resolving each of these in conjunction with the team. They may already know the solution, or have ideas for one. (I decided to merge the calendars.)

4) Follow up to see the plan is implemented. (Merge complete.)

5) Follow up to see the reason is eliminated. (No way to miss an appointment now.)

6) Follow up to see the problem is resolved
   – no new issues have occurred. Project is
   on course / mistake is eliminated.
   (I didn't stand her up the next time, and
   the next time, and the next….)

Summary

We all have blind spots. If she had not called me, I might
not have realized what I did until I looked at the calendar
again. Your team may not see the issue until you bring it up.
It's bad when it happens, but it happens. People forget, and
things get overlooked. Mistakes are made. The important
thing is to figure out how to prevent them from happening
again.

Don't get frustrated. Instead, get to the crux of the issue, and
improve the system.

Happy Leading!
Jean

5 Keys to a Productive Team

A neighbor once commented about how the guys (hubby and our two sons) tackled the front yard. He compared it to a military movement. They could really get a lot done in a short amount of time, and they all moved in sync!

If you've ever watched teams of folks work together – even ball teams, you cannot help but notice a few things.

1. Fun

Most of the day is spent with the folks at work – more than with their family. Your team will be much more productive if they can "play" throughout the day. I'm not talking about lots of breaks. I'm talking about a playful mindset or attitude and treating others like family. It makes for a better work environment if folks don't feel like they must always be serious, intense, and full of stress.

2. Rest

Studies have shown again and again that 40 hours is the optimal work week. In many cases, folks who worked longer were not any more productive. In fact, they became less productive. – Vacations are also important.

Breaks during work? Research is mixed about how productive they are. Personally, I'm more productive when I change tasks as I hit a snag. While I'm working on another task, the answer will come to me. You might find that true for your team too.

3. Attitude

Encourage an attitude of teamwork. When team members are supportive, everything becomes easier. That's why the guys could quickly tackle the front yard. They all knew what they needed to do, and how / when they needed to do it as a help to the rest of the team.

4. Organization

If you've ever had to spend time looking for a misplaced object, or clean up before you could actually start a project, you'll understand this one. When everything is in its place, productivity soars.

5. Cleanliness

Keep the work environment clean and free of debris. This can be a health and safety issue, but it can also save time just as organization saves time.

6. Bonus: Industrial engineering, ergonomics, and the like

Industrial engineers are the folks that determine how far apart to place the drive thru windows to make the process of ordering at fast food restaurants even faster. Small companies can increase productivity by thinking about the environment and workflow in this way. Start by taking a look at the layout of the workspace. Get feedback from the team for improvements. They can tell you what slows them down, and what they find frustrating. You may find that another piece of equipment can solve a bottleneck in production, or that a different order of tasks would make the workflow smoother.

Summary

Fun, rest, attitude, organization, cleanliness, and applying industrial engineering / ergonomics can make your team more productive. Take time to experiment and measure the results as you work to improve your team's productivity!

Happy Leading!
Jean

Leaders Take a Stand

Online and via email, I've been called a plethora of unkind things either outright or via insinuation. I've even lost a few online friends and old acquaintances.

Why?

It obviously was not just because of my beliefs and opinions. Most of these folks engaged me in conversation. However, when they found out that I would not change my mind, most – if not all – would proceed to badger me. Next, they would jump to name calling, insults, and / or false accusations. Then, they would unfriend me.

Have you ever had that happen to you? Maybe it wasn't online.

First, let me encourage you to remember that just because they have a different opinion, it doesn't make them right, and changing your mind to agree with them just because they act badly is not leadership.

Second, let me encourage you to always respect the opinions of others. They have the right to have an opinion - even if you don't agree with it. Acting badly just because they do not agree with you is also not leadership.

Third, anytime you are confronted, you have only two choices. You can take a stand for what you believe, or you can retreat. Caveat: If you find you really are on the wrong side of an opinion or belief, change sides immediately. Note: If you are seeking to please others, know that retreating is no guarantee of popularity.

When You Choose to Lead

Leaders must not be thin skinned. Leaders must lead. If you cease to share your thoughts or cease to speak up, you are not leading. Leaders do not lead to be liked. Leaders lead to change situations and outcomes.

Patton was a leader. So was MacArthur. They both knew how to rally folks behind them. They both stood for what they believed. Both had their enemies. Neither let opinion hold them back.

True leadership is knowing what to do and having the courage – perhaps the wisdom – to do it.

Summary

Leaders stand for what they believe. We all want to be liked, but changing your stand to please others is no guarantee of popularity. While flip-flopping usually gains you nothing, when you stand for what you believe, at the very least you can be happy with yourself!

Disclaimer: In the news, we hear of many events where leaders died for their beliefs. That's a choice you have to make for yourself. You always have the choice to follow instead of lead.

Happy Leading!
Jean

Use the Power in Your Words

Do you utilize the power you have in your words?

Have you ever told a story to 2 different people and used slightly different word choices in the process? We all do that. I'm not talking about lying, but I'm talking about the choice between two similar words. The choice can color – often unintentionally – what you are conveying.

I've seen folks get upset when I said something because they thought I was implying something that I was not implying. Sometimes it was my phrasing, and sometimes it was their perspective.

Leaders understand the power of their words and how to use that power.

Level 1 – The Power of Relationships

Much has been written about the power of relationships. If you network, those whom you have built relationships will often give you referrals. That's the focus of networking groups. Part of the equation is also trust and credibility.

What you must realize is that what you say plays into the success of that relationship. It's in your words.

Think about the relationships you have with family. Just because they know who you are gives you an edge. It can also hurt you if your words are not wise. Either way, you have some ability to get these folks to consider what you advise. These folks will think about your ideas.

Level 2 – The Power of Being the Influencer

You know that you've reached this point when folks pause to get your opinion. You may achieve it via experience, wisdom, talent, or perceived ability. You can use the power of your words to reach an extended audience because people begin to share your opinion with others. They may even reference you when they do. You are being talked about, and your words influence people beyond your immediate circle. Be sure to use your words for good.

Level 3 – The Power of Being the Expert

This level is the most fun and the most challenging. With it comes great responsibility.

At this level, your name and ideas grow way beyond your friends and the folks they know. Often folks know your name in the field even if they don't know your ideas. Conversely, they may also know your ideas and quotes even if they don't know much about you. Folks follow you because of reputation, and share your ideas because of value.

Summary

As your level of expertise grows, so does your influence. The more influence you have, the greater your ability to make things happen or at least influence them. The power of your words can bring you more business, influence the choices of others, and change your world.

Be responsible and enjoy the power of your words!

Happy Leading!
Jean

Intentionally Leave a Legacy

Are you aware that you have a legacy?

Your legacy?

If you are thinking that you don't have one, you are mistaken. We all do. It's what you've changed or affected that would have been left undone – at least for the time being – if it had not been for you.

Legacies come in many forms. Of course your children are your legacy. But what else have you left?

When we talk about leaving a legacy, we tend to think of famous folks like Columbus and George Washington. We may think of Paul Revere or Louis Pasteur. We seldom think of the folks who taught and inspired them – and we may not think much about our own.

You can be sure that you are leaving a legacy somewhere - in every person you touch, and in every action you take. Your legacy continues on.

Why do I care?

This is the heart of the issue.

An alcoholic tends to have alcoholic children. That's part of that person's legacy. That's not a legacy most of us would choose. Leaders care what their legacy looks like. They accept the responsibility of making sure the change they make is for the good.

Presidents often consider their own legacy – especially in their last few years in office. It's important to them to be remembered by history in a positive way. Not all succeed.

Whether you'd like to be remembered or not, you will be remembered if only by family and friends for what you have left behind in memories – good or bad.

Where and how?

Your legacy could be with your family and friends, but it could also be with your co-workers, acquaintances, and the world.

Any advice, inspiration, improvements, discoveries, processes, or cures are part of a legacy. Again, every life you touch and course of action you change is part of your legacy. When thinking about your own, think bigger than what you can see.

Although you may not get great credit for it, like a chain of dominos toppling, you set something in motion every day.

Summary

Consider your legacy. Are you intentionally leaving one? What do you think it looks like? What do you want to leave behind?

Happy Leading!
Jean

Developing New Leaders

If you are the owner, it will be obvious to you why you need to develop new leaders in your organization. What if you aren't the owner? Aren't the folks under you a threat? – I hope you don't see them that way. Some leadership experts say that the best leaders train their successors. They are right.

I hope you see that developing a new leader to run things in your absence frees up your time to work on other things, is good for the organization in the long run, and enables you to move up the ladder.

If you are viewed as too valuable in your current position, you will miss opportunities. Would you rather have someone say, "I can't take you from your current position because no one will be able to . . . ", or would you rather hear, "Let x take over while you train for the next level up"?

Choosing a New Leader

It takes time to choose and groom a new leader. In both stages, you will need to pay attention to decision making skills, people skills, and management (of things) skills. All these can be taught and learned, but it takes time.

Don't count someone out because of youth. Because of today's technology, many played games online as part of a team, or ran an online business from a very early age. Hence, they often have advanced their leadership skills before ever officially entering the marketplace.

Developing the New Leader

Three things a new leader has to have: responsibility, authority, and empowerment.

The way folks learn is through being given responsibility. The new leader cannot be let loose with it at first. Remember it's a process. Start small and build up.

In order to be successful and grow into this new responsibility, the leader also needs to feel empowered to make decisions concerning it. Again, go slow. Bad decisions are costly. Keep your eyes on the decisions. As the leader increases in decision making skills and knowledge, consider increasing what that area of responsibility encompasses.

Finally, the leader needs the authority to enforce / carry out the decisions. If you ever have to put the brakes on a decision, be sure to explain why, and if possible let that person correct any needed course of action. This is reassuring.

DISCLAIMER: You – not me – are responsible for how you use what I have just said. You can toss some folks into the deep end of the pool, and they will swim. Others will drown and drown you too if you try to save them. Remember not to toss someone in too quickly, and remember to stand back if you need to toss the proverbial life preserver.

Summary

Choose that new leader well, and then go slow as you develop them. Pay attention to detail as you go along because you will find that one of the most challenging jobs you will ever have is people development. However, it's also one of the most rewarding.

Happy Leading!
Jean

Set Them Up to Win

Several times in my life, a leader set me up to win. Each time it was done in such a way that it was obvious to me that it was a gift to jump start my success. Why was that done? What did that look like?

In one instance, I needed to charter a group for an organization. I had no idea how to find the people to start such a group (that came later), but a leader gave me two groups to work with that were early in process. The groups still needed to grow, and I still had to do my part. In the end, both chartered!!

Because I was able to dive in right away, my stress over the process was eliminated, and I achieved overall and continued success quicker than I otherwise would have.

Consider real estate. What if you were a new agent, and someone had you come along to a meeting to take your first listing? Finding a listing could take a while, but being given one right away allows you to see the process sooner. And when you sell a listing, you will have seen both sides. That would leave you to concentrate on finding listings without stressing over the remainder of the process. Your early experience – hopefully including sales and reward of commissions – will boost your confidence.

Setting a person up to win is sometimes more than training, manuals, and other tools. It's often more than walking a person through a task. Sometimes it's letting the person walk into the middle of a multi-task process that has a good chance – and not necessarily a guarantee - of succeeding.

Any long process can be examined to find the best entry point to set someone up to win. The key is that the person still needs to see and work most of the process and know that both success and failure are possible. In the end, assuming success, that person will have gained valuable knowledge and confidence.

Summary

I was given two groups in process. When you set someone up to win, you are not guaranteeing that it will happen. Either of those groups could have failed. Actually, they both could have. The set up was in the fact that I had opportunities given to me – two of them. If either succeeded, I would have felt successful.

It's important that you realize that setting someone up to win isn't about guaranteeing the outcome is a success, but rather that the opportunity is there.

Happy Leading!
Jean

Give Them the Credit

When I was in my 20s, I went fishing a lot. One day, after fishing for hours, my line went zipping out. I had a king mackeral on the other end! It was the fish that I was after. Someone else took my rod and landed my fish. I don't think I even got to play it a little. I was so disappointed.

This person took my fun away. I didn't have the success I had hoped. Instead, that person did. I didn't get the credit or even shared credit. He did. I didn't get to tell a fish tale. He did. Why was I even there?

Perhaps he needed the win more than me, but that left me wondering if I'd ever have success at catching a king mackeral. If I hooked another, would that be taken too? With no win, no credit, no story, and no fun, my enthusiasm was severely dampened.

What do you think or feel about the person who took my fish? When you see a team or a person about to succeed, let them. Then give the credit to that team or person. It makes you look great!

BTW, if you claim the credit, you take the reward. If you take the reward, you nullify the incentive to work hard. Future results will not be there. The thought will always remain that you might take the credit again. Even if you don't, it will take a long time for the memory to go away . . . Although I may not remember all the details of that event, I still remember that fish and how I felt over 25 years ago.

Summary

Your reputation suffers when you take unearned credit for something. In addition, any time you prevent a team or a person from succeeding, you are taking the achievement and the credit away. It might only be a small thing, but you don't know how much it might mean to someone.

Motivate your team and others by letting them have the win and giving them credit!

Happy Leading!
Jean

Articulate the Vision

I've seen and heard people in leadership roles express opinions that were in direct competition with the vision of the organization they represented. In some cases the person had not bought into the vision. In other cases the person was in major disagreement with the vision or mission at hand. While honesty is a great thing, the time to have recognized this difference was before assuming the role.

It's hard to be a great leader if you are not passionate about the vision you represent because it directly affects your attitude toward success. If you are aiming at a different target, you may be successful at that vision, but not the one at hand. Similarly, your team cannot be passionate if you are not expressing the vision in an understandable way, and typically, they will only be as passionate as you are.

In business, you will receive referrals according to what you articulate. If you articulate that you are cheap, that will draw a certain clientele. If you articulate that you are cutting-edge, that will attract a different clientele. It's the same when leading a team.

Since the team is watching you, your actions must fall in line with what you are articulating. The old cliché "walk the talk" holds true. What you do will stick with your team longer than what you say. If you don't follow the vision, it sends the message that the vision is not important, or it leads them toward the wrong vision.

Summary

If your team isn't following your vision, perhaps they don't have a clear understanding of what that is. Be sure you can express it well, and be sure you are living it out. It's also a great idea to post the vision where all can see.

If you are looking to create a vision and / or mission statement, world-class companies often post theirs online. Coca-Cola's is my favorite.

Happy Leading!
Jean

What Not to Delegate

If you have the gift of helps and you like to help others, you may have noticed that not everyone reciprocates. It's because most folks tend to focus on themselves, and what they need. Sometimes the need is simply that great. At other times, it's because they are takers.

What does this have to do with business and delegating? Everything.

Whether it's your company, your team, or simply your job, no one is going to love the company, team, or job like you do. Therefore, you cannot delegate everything.

You Cannot Delegate Responsibility

What if, for example, you have someone else assigned to do the invoicing, and they fail to do it? It could be that the workload coming in has become great, or it could be that they wanted to take off and go to the ballgame with the kids. It might be that person's responsibility to mail an invoice, but that person is not responsible for the health of the company. Although the two connect, this is often today's thinking – or perhaps lack of understanding. What happens if the invoicing doesn't get done for weeks?

I'm not saying that you should not delegate certain tasks. I am saying that delegating it and it getting done are not the same thing. Follow it to completion. Make sure the tasks get done.

You Cannot Delegate Passion

Embrace the fact that others are not going to be as passionate about your dream or vision as you are. It won't matter what you've asked them to do, it will be done in a less enthusiastic way than if you had done it yourself. Your only solution here is to choose carefully those you ask, and pay attention to how passionate – or not – that person seems to be about the task. Leave the less passionate behind. The lack of enthusiasm affects results.

You Cannot Delegate Expertise

Sometimes, folks just want you to do the job. Your reputation is a blessing, and it can make you in demand. I recently wanted a certain photographer. She just could not do it in the timeframe that I needed, and she offered to delegate to another photographer. The photos turned out great, but it was a hard sell because I had spent a lot of time researching local photographers.

When expertise is involved, you can still delegate, but more often than not you will have to remain involved or at least appear to have your hand on it in order to have the result be acceptable to the requestor. Be sure to try to delegate to someone who will get similar or better results than you would if you kept the task yourself.

Summary

While you can delegate just about anything, certain things cannot be delegated. Your responsibility, your passion, and your expertise are three things that cannot ever be delegated to others. Those belong to you!

Happy Leading!
Jean

Finding Value in the Failures

Right after Bob and I married, I got a job selling businesses. It paid commission, and it led to my taking real estate classes. When an unresolvable situation arose, I quit the job. By the time I got my real estate license, I was pregnant, and sometimes, my morning sickness lasted all day.

I had planned to talk to a broker about working under him. He took one look at me, and with little conversation said he was only willing to take me on if I could work 40 hours a week. With morning sickness lasting all day several days a week, I could not guarantee it.

My end result: a real estate license and no job. Eventually, after scoping out some daycares, I decided to be a stay at home mom.

What did I accomplish with all that? On the surface, it looked like a waste of time, energy, and money. In reality, it was a very informative experience.

First, I learned a lot about myself. I don't enjoy cold calling – in person or on the phone, and I was not very effective at it.

That information has helped me with future endeavors. I also read my first Zig Ziglar book during this time.

Second, I learned a few things about others. Business owners can make some pretty interesting decisions and comments – some of which I may not ever understand.

Third, I learned that I could not be happy dropping my child into the care of another. He'd be sick more often, and he wouldn't be cared for the way that I'd care for him. Since I had options, I opted out. It took this experience to move me to that place.

Fourth, I learned something about both real estate and selling businesses that I would be able draw from later on.

Summary

Not every failed on-the-surface adventure is really a failure. Life changing moments are often found in the journey. Something can always be learned. The gain may be greater than the loss, and time will prove it out.

Happy Leading!
Jean

Avoid Busy Work

It's easy to get caught up in doing things a certain way just because everyone else does them that way, or because we have always done them that way. If we are not careful, we can easily create busy work for ourselves and for our team.

Two Examples

In the past, I have enjoyed printing some of the envelopes to my Christmas cards on my printer. When I purchased a new printer, I discovered that I could not easily get it to work with the envelopes I had purchased. By the time I gave up, I could have handwritten the addresses. This year, I went for the simple solution.

I sell a lot online. When I first started, I was not putting the lot number in the listings . . . and I have a lot of lots that I'm splitting out to sell. Later, by adding this simple detail, I could go straight to the right box to retrieve it for shipping.

Summary

Simple, small changes can sometimes save a lot of time. In order to find those changes, you must look at each process.

Every task has a purpose and a reason, and the way it's being done should complement that. Sometimes processes need to be improved because of growth. Sometimes the way something is being done has never really been the best solution, or an innovation has come along.

Be sure to also get your team's input. They may have solutions that you haven't considered. Challenge them to think in terms of scalability.

Happy Leading!
Jean

Talk is NOT Action:
A Trap We ALL Land In

"Talk is not action" is a phrase that would get a "DUH" from most folks. However, most folks fall into this trap without realizing it. It's easy to want to progress to another level. It's easy to know that there are things that you don't know, and then go in search of the training for you or your team.

The Hard Part – The Trap

The trap is that it's possible to get stuck in the preparation or training phase. Sometimes we don't take the next step because of fear; it may be the fear of the unknown. Sometimes that unknown can only be realized by taking the step. What a cycle!

I had been designing my own website when a family member suggested that I start a business building websites. I was scared that I'd get in over my head, and I started with very simple sites. I also knew who to call to bail me out if I needed it.

Not every business is easy to ease into. You can easily get yourself into a jam if you don't know the risks, licensing requirements, insurance requirements, costs, etc. connected to what you want to do. Hence, I'm not suggesting that you move too fast on your next plan – business or otherwise. What I am suggesting is that there will come a point in your learning and research where you really aren't learning anything new – or not enough to stay at that level. There comes a time to move on.

My speaking and coaching business is like that. For years I spoke as opportunities came my way. Finally, I realized that to make the dream of speaking into the big reality that I wanted, I had to stop talking about what I wanted to do and just go do it.

The Big Myth

I went from speaking for an organization to not speaking to realizing how much I missed it to wanting to make it as a full time speaker on my own. It was at this point that I thought I needed to find the door to the speaking world. Although my skills needed some honing, the myth is that you have to find a door. It's like thinking that you want to be an actress, but you have to be discovered to make it.

Although training and practice is needed, it's really about marketing and sales.

The myth is whatever lie we believe about why we aren't more successful at doing what we want to do. It's more than the trap of preparing; it's looking for something that doesn't exist. I was looking for a door.

Summary

The trap is thinking you need more preparation then you do. The big myth is anything that you believe exists when it really doesn't, and you believe that it needs to happen for you to be successful. It hides the path to success. You won't succeed until you start the journey. Talk is not action. And action is not profitable action if it doesn't move you closer to achieving your goal.

Take a closer look at what you believe about preparation and myths similar to what I mentioned. You might find you are closer to success then you thought.

Happy Leading!
Jean

Your Team May Bring More to the Table Than You Think

Easy to Assume Incorrectly Because of Background

"Jean, I didn't know that you knew WordPerfect," was the essence of what was said.

He was surprised because I was a young homemaker who could easily pass for being even 10 years younger, and I would seem to have no need of this information. It would have been easy to assume that I had married right out of high school.

Easy to Assume Incorrectly Because of Age

When Robbie was 12 or maybe 13, we visited a museum where there was a child size airplane complete with cockpit. It might have been a ride. I don't remember, but it had controls that looked like the real thing. Robbie crawled up into it and started talking about what each lever did. Bob (my hubby and his dad) was surprised by what Robbie knew. – Computer flight games are so real!

Always Ask

Often folks will have hidden talents, abilities, and training to bring to the table that can really help your team achieve success. You won't discover these if you make assumptions. The correct approach would be to get to know the backgrounds of each team member, and always ask, "Does anyone have this ability?" You might be surprised.

Summary

In the past folks stuck to the same career path their entire life. This is no longer the case. I once met a man that was interested in selling businesses. He said he had been a pilot. What a career swap! And with the internet so readily available, you never know what someone has researched or what hobby they may have. The whole world is at our fingertips.

Knowing and relying on the talents and skills of your team can save time and money by making outsourcing or additional research optional. It can speed processes and enhance your products and services.

Happy Leading!
Jean

Reasons to Avoid Using
Bad Language With Your Team

The greatest potential I have for regularly hearing offensive language would be the television. I don't like the bad language; therefore, I don't watch very many of the newer shows. For the most part, I stick to news commentaries and the shows that predate the 1980s. My favorite channel is "OFF."

Your Team Might Tune You Out

As a leader, you want your message to get through to your team. Just as I physically tune out the television or choose to selectively watch, your team may choose to tune out or selectively listen to you if your language is not up to par.

Worse than that, they may not tell you.

Your Reputation Could Suffer

Consider all the ways you may use offensive language. If you use it to jump on someone who is having issues, it's uncaring.

If you pitch a fit, it can be intimidating. If you just think you have a right to swear, and so you will, you could be considered disrespectful. Perhaps you are thinking that you use bad language to be funny or get attention. Are you not more creative than that?

I Am Who I Am

I was at a meeting where a speaker used over the top language. I had paid to be there, and fortunately he was called out. What if I had wanted to hire him to coach me? What if I had wanted to hire him to speak for another group? I would not. If the argument can be made that he is who he is, then I would not be interested in subjecting myself or others to his brand.

Not everyone may feel that way, but it's a deal breaker to many.

Summary

As noted, bad language is offensive and can come off as being uncaring, intimidating, and disrespectful. Your reputation and your business may suffer as people may view that as your brand, and it makes you look less credible.

Before you choose your words, consider the consequences and choose wisely.

Happy Leading!
Jean

The Value of Talking with the Team - Not at Them

Do You Feel the Need to Bark Out Orders?

When Robbie was 3 years old, we went to visit relatives who were having an outdoor celebration. I was asked to film parts of the event. Bob (my hubby and the boys' dad) had the job of helping watch Robbie – who was extremely active. A grandparent was in charge of holding Drew.

When we stepped out of the car, I realized that their rather large yard was situated on a well-traveled road. I looked at Robbie and said, "Stay out of the road. If a car hits you, there will be no more Robbie."

Later, I saw Robbie following his uncle. I did not think as they walked right by me that the uncle might walk out into the road and keep going without a thought about what Robbie might do. (The uncle may or may not have even realized Robbie was right behind him.) Moments later, the uncle was in the road, and Robbie stopped at the edge of the yard.

Parents know that when raising children, they need them to be compliant. Stay out of the street is not a request. It's an order!

Likewise, military commanders know that in times of emergency, it's important to have a well-trained team who will follow orders without asking questions. Conversation can cost lives.

At work . . . Well, now that's a different story.

Leading people is not about giving orders or talking at them. There may be times when it's critical and you may have to give an order. Hopefully your team will understand that. It's important for you to understand that the team wants you to talk with them. They crave discussion, and they want to be able to make decisions for themselves.

Trust the Team

Trusting the team to make the best decisions is risky, or is it?

The ability to trust the team begins with the course of the discussions you have with them. Begin by giving the team a choice between good options. No matter what they choose, the team wins.

Then, discuss the responsibilities and the expectations for each task. Give each member as much freedom as possible to achieve the desired results. Remember, the more freedom the team has, the more they own the result.

The easiest type of freedom to give is the freedom of creativity. For example, you may need a sign with certain information on it. Instead of telling the team what to do, let the team design the sign.

Summary

Talking at the team achieves little. No one likes being bossed. Additionally, members of the team may feel that their ideas were not valued, and a better solution existed.

The value of talking with the team is trust. Discussion leads to each member knowing what needs to happen, assuming responsibility for certain tasks, and being given the freedom to be creative in performing those tasks and making the necessary decisions. Hence, each member will own the result.

Happy Leading!
Jean

Challenging Your Team
Through Competition

Is competition always a good thing? Does everyone want to compete?

These two questions are the foundation for how you motivate a team. The answers to them might not be as intuitive as you might think.

Is competition always a good thing?

Yes, but not all competitions are a good thing. Some competitions achieve unwanted results.

Churches have been known to run competitions to see which class can get the most visitors. It can be argued that the real goal should be to win folks to Christ not grow membership, but I digress . . .

Competition between clearly defined classes can work out well. If visitor Sally is in the 6th grade, then Sally's class would get the credit. If it's competition between members, that's better. The 4th grader who bought Sally would get the credit. Hence, Sally gets invited as opposed to the 4th grader considering if she wants to help the 6th grade class win.

What happens when the competition is between less than clearly defined adult classes? If someone comes in the door, who grabs that visitor? The singles class? The men's class? Another adult class? You see, competition not clearly thought out can quickly sour and may even result – especially in the business world – in backstabbing to get ahead. For competition to work well, there must not be any hindrances to folks wanting to participate. They must have a clear goal, and they must have a reason to work toward that goal. What is the reward? A larger class? A pizza party?

Does everyone want to compete?

Yes, probably, but not like you might think.

I reached a point in my life where I did not need to win. I like to win, but I did not need to prove anything by winning. Hence, winning was optional, and I was not passionate about it. What was important to me was to compete with myself. My goals were intrinsic.

Some folks do not like competitions between members in a group. I was stunned when I first heard this because I find competitions fun although often the subjective nature of some (like performances) can be a bit confusing when you don't agree with the results.

Summary

Competition can be a great way to challenge your team to do better. Effective competitions are the ones where the rules are clear, and the rewards are well stated. The best competitions, however, are when folks compete with their previous performance. These must start with a baseline. That baseline can be set with a measure of recent performance before the contest starts. Example: You turned out 100 widgets last month. When teams or individuals compete with a previous performance, it's good to have a discussion about where they see improvements can be made in process. Make the tweak, try again, and measure results. This gives them the feedback needed to know if the tweak made a difference.

Happy Leading!
Jean

How Do You Know
When You've Arrived at Success?

At the end of an event that I thought went well, the director above me made the comment that we needed to define what success looks like.

He had a point.

I've done many things that I thought were successful, but it's easy to get caught up in the fun. If you don't know the purpose or goal of what you are doing, how do you know when you've arrived at success?

Now, years later, as I plan my own events, I'm setting goals that will measure success. The goals are very specific. For example:

- How many folks do I want in the room?
- What outcomes do I want for these folks, and how will I measure that?
- How interactive do I want to make it?

It's more than promote and hope. It's more than design a program by a certain time. It's not about meeting deadlines. It's about measuring the results of everything that went into the planning and preparation and being able to determine what worked and what didn't.

In order to know that, you must know specifically what it looks like before you start. In my example, 30 people in the room who participate, learn, and then give lots of positive feedback would be a good indication of success.

Would it be success to have 5 people in the room who had fun, learned little, and went away unclear and unsupported? Nope. However, if you had 5 folks in the room who had fun, but did not give you any feedback, you'd be in the dark about the success concerning even those 5. You might think since they had fun that it was successful. That's not necessarily so. It could also be argued that even if only 5 were in the room, and the rest of the results were good that the event had a measure of success.

Summary

Whatever you are going to do, you must have the list of things you want to achieve and a way built in to measure those. At the end of the day, measuring success will give you a clearer picture of whether or not you were really successful.

Happy Leading!
Jean

Know the Dreams of the Individuals on the Team

Pot luck is the scariest term anyone can use around me. The thought of cooking for an event is enough to discourage me and possibly keep me from going. When I'm in the kitchen situations that involve fire alarms, broken glass, and shattered plates happen way too often. I'm much more at home with a small battery powered chainsaw, drill, or hammer.

Let's suppose you want to plan an event with your team. You put some folks in charge of planning the food and others in charge of decorating which would require building an arch. You decide to let the ladies be in charge of the food, and the men in charge of building. See a problem?

Instead, what if you knew the dreams of your team? One teammate might be trying to get into culinary. Another might want to be an event planner. This event could go to a whole new level by relying on the skills and talents of the team that go beyond the workplace.

Not only would you benefit, but the folks who handled the food and the planning have added to their resume. This is a built in bonus for them. It could be more valuable than any cash bonus you could give them because it could further their careers by opening other doors of opportunity.

Would this cost you an employee? No. Okay, so they might be able to get another job because of the assistance you just gave them, but they were looking in that direction anyway. However, they will also speak good things of you and your company.

Summary

Knowing the dreams of the folks on your team not only benefits you, but it will allow you to reward them with opportunities to grow. These opportunities could be within the company or not. Either way, it shows you care about them and not just what they can do for you. It leads to better relationships and happier teammates.

Happy Leading!
Jean

The Result of Showing Appreciation

I said thank you to the lady on the other side of the counter at the post office. She had just said thank you to me. She in turn asked me why I said thank you. I told her it was for doing her job and doing it well.

I have to admit that I would not always have told someone thank you in a situation that looks like they should be telling me thank you. After all, I was the customer. She was doing what she gets paid to do. No extra effort was needed. Most folks would have answered, "You're welcome."

When is the last time you got waited on poorly? I bet it wasn't that long ago. Maybe a few more expressions of gratitude would be enough to encourage folks to do a little better or to keep doing their best.

Summary

Consider the last business meeting you attended. Did not the words (and the way they were said) during the opening of the meeting set the tone for the rest of the meeting?

Consider the tone set by a welcome versus words of appreciation versus a scolding.

Sometimes the mood of a whole team can be affected by the mood of one person. When you brighten one person's day, you may brighten the day of your whole team.

Your words have power. Use them wisely.

Happy Leading!
Jean

Celebrate Success

When we were children, our parents often celebrated our successes. We may have had birthdays with cakes, a sweet sixteen party, a trophy for doing well at an event, certificates at the end of a school year, and / or any number of other rewards and celebrations along the way.

Some companies bring in food or take their folks out to eat after a big success. Others put on even bigger celebrations when it's appropriate.

When Should You Celebrate?

It's important to celebrate successes as they come along because folks feel rewarded and appreciated for their contribution to the success. They may also benefit personally because for some they associate their self-worth with their job (not that they should). Hence, it touches them deeply. I'm not suggesting that you reward folks to manipulate them, but I am suggesting that it could be appreciated more than you think.

How Much Do You Spend?

The celebration should always be comparable to the success achieved. A day of hard work might be rewarded with pizza delivery, but a month of hard work that landed a $60,000 per year contract would probably merit a party or at the very least a nice dinner out and / or bonus. The bigger the achievement, the bigger the celebration.

Who Do You Reward?

Have you ever seen someone in a sports event get a trophy for participation? If you can get a trophy for participating, doesn't that devalue the winning positions? Doesn't it make finishing first less of a goal?

If you work in a large company, quite often you will see a department get rewarded with a celebration or a bonus instead of the whole company. This really makes sense. You would not appreciate a reward for work that you did not do. Yes, it might be fun, but it doesn't encourage you to repeat a success because it wasn't your success.

Summary

To make the most impact, celebrations that are used as a reward for success must be done consistently as each achievement occurs, be proportional in size to the achievement, and be specific to the person or team who earned it.

Tip: If you celebrate with one team for their success, be sure to let the other teams you lead know the reason that team got to celebrate. This prevents them from thinking you are playing favorites and helps them to see what they can do to also be able to celebrate. Then, be sure to reward them when they succeed.

Happy Leading!
Jean

Keep Relationships Up-To-Date

I had a friend that needed an ear. She was not the first, nor will she be the last. I didn't mind, but I did notice that a lot of what she had to say was from her perspective. The other person, although often in the wrong according to her side of the story – and some things are black and white, seemed at times to be guilty of . . . well . . . breathing.

Okay, I'm exaggerating. However, human nature is that when we like someone that person can do no wrong, and when we don't like someone that person can do no right. Do you think that is realistic? The truth often lies somewhere in the middle, but perspectives are influenced by feelings of fear and anger.

I once was so angry and frustrated by someone that I made the statement that this person wasn't going to stop until . . . My listener asked, "Did he say that?" He had not said it, but my emotions were in full swing. My mind was spinning, and I felt for a moment that it was his intent – even though it was not.

You may have heard the old cliché about rose colored glasses and the saying about not going to bed angry. Ephesians tells us, "let not the sun go down upon your wrath." A lot of truth lies behind all of these because time usually doesn't make hurt feelings or anger better. It usually makes them worse.

Summary

As a leader, if you are angry at someone, you will tend to view that person in a negative way. You may not give them the opportunities that they deserve. This is not only unfair to that person, but it casts you in a poor light as well. In short, it can affect your judgment and your reputation. It also means that you may miss out on the gifts and talents that person can bring to the equation.

Be sure to confront peaceably and with a cool, level head a situation before emotions have the opportunity to smolder.

Happy Leading!
Jean

Keep Your Eye on the Tone of the Team

I was part of a team where all the members came together in mission and vision except one. He refused to comply to the standards the team wanted to uphold. In addition, his attitude became intolerable, and he made waves.

I've seen variations of this again and again. When a team member refuses to move and act in the same direction as the rest of the team, it can make it impossible for the team to succeed. At the very least it slows the team down. In some cases, it can make the work environment unbearable.

Please note that I'm not talking about folks who simply have different ideas. I'm talking about folks who are undermining decisions that have been made.

What Should You Do?

First, you need to know and abide by the parameters as set by law and your organization for how to proceed. However, a typical approach would be to start with a conversation. Sometimes that will clear up any confusion. If the situation is serious enough, the person will have to be removed from the team.

It's important to remove law breakers, rule breakers, and other disrupters from the team because their influence can sour the whole group. If they are a respected member, try to find a way to have them exit gracefully to minimize the impact on the rest of the team.

What If You Have to Work with Them Anyway?

The hardest decision to make can be how to handle someone that you know is hurting a team when you can't remove that person because of the impact that will be left behind. Sometimes you must wait it out and hope for a team change. Other times, you must find a way to discredit the advice of this person enough to change the perspective of the rest of the team.

I'm not suggesting being dishonest. I am suggesting that if you know the person does not have the best interest of the group in mind that you may be able to show that in some way without having to actually say it. Research, fact-finding questions, and historical data can all be helpful.

If done correctly, you gain the respect of the group, and you don't have to do anything that brings harm to the other person financially or otherwise. (This keeps you out of court.) You don't want to make the person look bad, you just want to show the error of their thinking. You seek to bring truth and harmony.

Happy Leading!
Jean

A Good Leader Projects a Good Tone

As I recounted a story to Charles, one of our sons, he asked, "Why are you talking to me like that?"

I had not realized it, but as I recounted the story, I was partially reliving it and partially reacting to it. It was one of those situations where I handled it professionally when it happened, but the more I thought about it later, the more I wondered about the motive of the other person in the story.

My tone, particularly for my own dialogue, was reflecting my afterthoughts instead of what actually happened. When he first called me out, I didn't know what he was talking about. He had to imitate me to get his point across. Then, I had to explain I had not used that tone at the time.

My poor tone caused confusion. Between the two of us, it was easy to clear up, but if it had been at the top of a business meeting, I may not have been called out. The meeting could have continued on a bad note.

How to Start Your Meeting on a Great Note

Make a point to start meetings with an upbeat tone. Bring as much energy and enthusiasm as you can to the meeting.

When I'm the president, I like to start our Toastmasters meeting with, "Welcome to Burlington Toastmasters Club #1835. We've got an exciting meeting planned!"

Now, you might be thinking, "What if it's a night where attendance is down?" Then, I might say, "Welcome to Burlington Toastmasters Club #1835. We're a little thin tonight, but we're going to have a great time!"

When you start on a great note, the enthusiasm and energy will carry to the rest of the team and flavor the meeting.

Summary

Just as you can start a meeting on a sour note or a great one, your tone affects the perception of the team in every situation. Their perception is their reality. You'll find that most of the time a happy tone means a happy team.

Happy Leading!
Jean

Help Others Get Back Up

If you have ever made a mistake and your boss jumped up and down and pitched a royal fit, then you know what that feels like. Have you ever seen that done to a group of folks?

I have, and it leaves them exasperated and temporarily unproductive. If someone cries, that person is out of work for the next 20 minutes or so. If extremely upset, that person could leave for the rest of the day and perhaps not return at all.

A Better Solution

When a mistake has been made, it is necessary to address it. In most cases your team will be harder on themselves than you are on them. A great way to address an issue is to start with the resulting error, and then work backwards to correct it.

When the bill I paid came back to me in the mail, I realized how hard I might have been on someone else if they made that same mistake. We can use that as an example.

Step 1: Show the issue. (My returned envelope with my payment for a bill.)

Step 2: Discuss any resulting damage. (Late fees, bad credit, etc. Fortunately, I still had time to be on time.)

Step 3: Ask, "Why was it done this way?" (I usually mail invoices to my clients in windowed envelopes. I took the invoice I received and stuffed it into a windowed envelope, which showed me as the recipient. I didn't notice. My goof!)

Depending on the answer to Step 3, you may wish to skip Step 4. If the team has had a really traumatic incident, it could increase the rate of errors because their minds are not on what they are doing. Human nature kicks in.

Step 4: Ask, "How can we keep this from happening again?" (Pay bills when I'm more wide awake and not in a hurry. Pay more attention to what I'm doing.)

Step 5: Be encouraging. (Sounds like I was just off my game, and I know my weaknesses. It could happen to anyone. I'll do better.)

Step 6: Monitor results. (I haven't done it again . . . At least not yet.)

As you can see, I was good to me! Be good to your team! The error needs to be addressed, but it doesn't have to be an event. It can be a checkup.

Summary

If mistakes are addressed correctly and with warmth, not only can you avoid tearing down a team, but you can help them recover from the misstep. Help them see that mistakes happen to all of us. The key is understanding why it happened so that it doesn't happen again.

Happy Leading!
Jean

Passionate About the Vision

Someone once told me, "Your eyes light up when you talk about Drew's Animals."

Of course my eyes light up. In many ways, DrewsAnimals. com is the third child. It started as a family homeschool project, and over the years I spent an enormous amount of time on it. We love the Lord, and we love our sons. Drew's Animals represents our family's heart for ministry. I can't help but be passionate about it.

Visions Are Bigger Than Goals

Although it all started with Drew's Animals, Drew's Animals isn't really the vision. The vision is to reach the world for Jesus. It's what our sons said that they wanted to do when we told them we wanted them to have a website. Drew's Animals is just one way to accomplish that.

I want to make a difference where I stand. It's my passion to change lives. One way I have chosen to express that is to help others be more successful. Business coaching, roundtable discussions, and workshops are all a part of that vision, and these things serve to open doors to share my faith either openly or via my books.

The Influence

Your passion influences your choices. When you are passionate about the vision you have for your team, project, or company, you'll find ways to make almost everything you do support the vision.

Your passion can also influence others. Just as the person I was talking with saw passion in my eyes, your passion will show too. It's the driving fire that will keep you going and encourage others to follow along if you let it show. Remember, enthusiasm is contagious!

Summary

Since the vision you have is carried forward on the passion you have for it, you need to choose a vision in line with your passion. When you do, you will have greater influence. As others see your passion, they will be encouraged to become a part of your vision.

Happy Leading!
Jean

Pay the Team What They Are Worth

Should the minimum wage be raised or even nearly doubled in some cases? When you raise the minimum wage, businesses will automate jobs, increase the work load on others, or raise prices because sometimes there just isn't that kind of profit in a job.

As a business owner, I can tell you that if I had to pay almost twice the current minimum wage, I would not consider hiring a teenager in most cases. Most teens simply do not have the skills to bring that kind of profit.

Now if that sounds like discrimination, it would not be because I really would need to include higher skills in the job description to get my money's worth. People want value when they purchase services. Companies must get value when they purchase services too, and that includes labor.

On the flip side, when you hire folks, you need to pay them what they are worth. It's become a practice today among larger corporations to hire contracting companies to manage certain parts of their businesses. This means that the folks the contractors hire wind up with less pay because the contractors need to make something too. That's understandable, but corporations also pay a price in the long run if they do not turn the more skilled workers into direct hires. After these folks get the training they need, they move on if salary doesn't follow. It's a tradeoff. The contractors take care of the turnover, but the corporation risks losing its better workers.

Summary

The market still works as long as there are other jobs out there. If you want to keep your best folks, pay them what they are worth in salary, benefits, and gratitude. When you do, they will bring you the skills you need for your company to be successful. Remember, training new folks is costly, and when you don't pay your better workers what they are worth, you will lose them to those who will.

Happy Leading!
Jean

Eliminate Bullying, Racism, & Drama

As a professional, you need professional folks working for you. Bullying, racism, and drama are time wasters, and in many cases are against the law and / or may be against your company's policies. You don't want to spend your time as a referee, and you don't want any lawsuits.

Train your folks to do a job, and then expect it to be done professionally and without a lot of yada yada. Creating this type of corporate climate should help prevent bad behavior because bad behavior will seem out of place instead of the norm.

What if it still occurs? Bullying, racism, and drama cannot be tolerated in the workplace. It's clear that if you permit it, there will be consequences. The least of these will be unhappy employees. For more serious offenses, there are laws in place to guide you. Your company also may have a procedure in place. Know your options.

I contract folks for a task on a project. If I don't like the behavior, I don't ask the person back, or I change the company that I've chosen for the job. You may not have that luxury.

Other ways to deal with bad behaviors on the job include scheduling the person for less hours, writing up the person which builds a case for later dismissal, help the person see that the job is not for him or her, or move the person physically to another spot in the workplace. Again, let your company policies and laws prevail. I can't give you a specific course of action, but I can tell you that it has to be stopped for the good of the company.

Summary

Set high standards designed to keep your employees happy and productive. Keep yourself and your company out of court by being sure all laws are followed. Have stated policies and procedure in place for dealing with bad behavior, and follow those policies.

Happy Leading!
Jean

Even Less Than Blunt
Can Hold You Back

The kids were growing up, and I decided to enter the business world again. I discovered quickly that not everyone appreciates straightforwardness. I'm not talking about being rude or hurtful. I'm talking about being honest in a direct way. Times have changed.

I'm the type of person that if I ask you how to improve something, I expect you to tell me several things that I can do to improve. Evidently, that's not what some folks want or need for feedback.

The conversation that is expected is one that is much longer. First, you must point out the positive. Then, you cannot go straight to the improvement point without finding a way to soften it, and then you must also wrap it in a positive so that no one mistakes it for judging. Phrases like "to make it even better" or "to make it more powerful" can be helpful here. Finally, you must summarize whatever it is you just said with something even more positive or perhaps forward looking.

Gone are the days of, "That's pretty cool. Have you tried x? I think it would be helpful." You are only allowed that among the more task oriented folks and among folks where you've gained their trust. If you are lucky that includes your family and closest friends.

Don't get me wrong. The constructive improvement point or points sandwiched between two positives is a great idea – and you should do that where applicable, but that improvement point has to be carefully crafted or the wheels just might fly off regardless of what you said before and after.

I quickly learned that the smile frozen on some folks' faces was not one of happiness. It was one of hurt feelings or anger. For a while it was inexplicable to me. What had I said?

I was expected to give feedback, and I wrapped it in positives, but that was not good enough.

Although there wasn't anything wrong with what I said or the tone I used, for whatever reason some folks today need to have extra-extra tender loving care when trying to help them. Be forewarned, if you don't use it, you may be accused of judging.

I battled with myself for a long time about the benefits of this in leadership. As a leader, should you have to sugarcoat absolutely everything? No, but it will make life simpler because you will have less hurt feelings among those you lead.

I still think it's their problem, but unfortunately, you have to deal with it.

Happy Leading!
Jean

Look for Ways to Foster Synergy

Ernest Hamwi created the first ice cream cone. He was selling waffles next to an ice cream vendor at the St. Louis World's Fair in 1904. The ice cream vendor ran out of containers, and Hamwi came to the rescue.

Now that's synergy. Another word for it is interdependency. In this case, what came out of the cooperation of the two was greater than either would have come up with on their own.

Interdepartmental meetings or meetings between teams can foster that kind of synergy if encouraged. Synergy can also form within teams, but the more varied the background the better the opportunity for synergy.

How to Encourage Synergy

Opportunities for networking and team building activities can go a long way toward fostering synergy because it enhances the opportunity to work together. Be sure though that the connection is drawn that the opportunity for this fun time to socialize or play together is also a time to bounce ideas off one another and seek solutions.

If the opportunity for solution seeking is not vocalized, then it could be missed. Set the stage by asking the folks to think about these questions.

- Who in another department might be able to help your workflow?
- Who in another department depends on your work flow?
- Wouldn't it be nice if there were a better or more efficient way to ……..?
- If you wanted to create something new for our customers, what would it be? Who can help with that?

Be sure the folks know that while this can be a fun time, it's also a time to introduce themselves and get to know the folks in the other department. If needed, the actual work of brainstorming can be reserved for a later meeting, but this is a time for them to set the stage and figure out the who and what for that meeting.

Summary

Synergy only happens where there's opportunity. It's encouraged during networking and team building activities, but it also hinges on good communication and often good relationships. Remember, folks who play together often work better together. However, the goal of achieving synergy may need to be expressly stated.

Happy Leading!
Jean

How to Prepare to Lead a Meeting

The first Girls in Action meeting that I led, I also invited parents. I put everything into folders and I had the folders nicely organized. I based my information on where my children were in their studies and my memory of my education.

During the meeting, I reached for something from one of the folders. I had not labeled the folders, so I fumbled. When the meeting was over, the parents and children were pleased, but one of the parents clued me in that not all the children could read yet.

Was I prepared for the meeting? Yes, and well, no. Not completely.

I had prepared the materials that I wanted to present, but I had over organized them into folders which as I said, I had not labeled. I had based my understanding of where the children were in their reading on other children instead of anticipating that some may not read yet.

I learned.

How to Prepare

- Know your audience.
- Know your topic.
- Confirm critical details in advance.
- Don't over organize.
- Practice by walking yourself through the presentation and actually doing it – not just rehearsing the words or points in your head.
- Practice using your visuals, if you have them.
- Anticipate questions.
- Have activities for the group to complete if you should need to step away, fix technology, etc.
- Always have more to present than you plan to present in case you get through the planned material quickly.

Summary

You can absolutely organize everything and still miss something. When you actually give the presentation as a part of your practice, you will discover many of those things. What if the technology doesn't work? What if the you reach for something, and you've left it in the car? Take steps to prepare for the unexpected.

Happy Leading!
Jean

Create Realistic But Challenging Expectations

If my goal were to sell a million widgets next week, would that happen? I suppose it could, especially if I had sold almost that many this week. Since I didn't, it would seem silly to expect that to happen. You could say, "DUH" right here.

While your dreams and aspirations for your team should always be huge because you'll ultimately go further if they are, your short term expectations need to be challenging, realistic, and achievable.

What if you set expectations too low?

With low expectations, either the team will be elated when they find out they have exceeded them, or they will be watching and may slack off as they approach the goal. In short, some folks may live down to that goal.

In either case, if you don't raise the next goal, you could be missing an opportunity to excel.

What if you set expectations too high?

Did the team barely miss, or were they way off the mark? If they barely missed, it could motivate them to work a little harder. It was probably an appropriate expectation. If they fell way short, it could frustrate them unless there is an obvious reason for the difference. Never achieving a goal creates a defeated attitude. A team will need a lot of encouragement when they miss the mark, especially if they thought they'd achieve it.

How do you set realistic expectations?

Historical data and observation will be the best benchmark for finding a starting point.

Ask yourself the following:

- What has been the average in the past?
- How hard did your team work to achieve that?
- What other factors were involved?
- What was done to help achieve the goal?
- What hindered the goal?

What if it's a new project?

If this is a new project, you may not have any way to set expectations. Focus on documentation. You'll want to be able to do exactly the same thing again in the future to create similar results. From there you can set expectations and tweak contributing factors.

Summary

Setting expectations can be a process, and getting them right is important. When you set them correctly, your team will feel challenged to achieve them, and they will feel accomplished when they do. High standards are a good thing. When you set them too low or way too high, your results will suffer.

Happy Leading!
Jean

Forecasting

Forecasting is more than setting expectations based on historical data. Forecasting involves looking into the future circumstances. It's similar to setting expectations for a goal, but it takes into account a bigger picture.

I use to market myself as a web designer for businesses owned by mom and pops. Those folks typically offered services or sold a small variety of products. I designed sites for them quickly and inexpensively, and I offered a small service plan. Over time, the web became more popular. Simple sites could be installed and updated by the user fairly easily. Then, more high tech sites became more user friendly. Ultimately, I started losing clients because the kid next door could throw together a site. Never mind that the kid next door knew nothing of SEO (search engine optimization), but I digress . . . The market started changing.

This left me two choices. I could step up my game and offer to do a higher level of coding that could involve security and a greater liability for me, or I could focus on something else that I may even love more. As you can tell, I chose the latter.

Forecasting involved looking at the future opportunities for my company. I determined what they were and how they affected me. You can do this inside of departments too.
In sales, you must look at the way you currently find and connect with your customers. Is this still the best way? In working with other departments or companies, you need to look at how you communicate with them. Do you still need to get on a plane or would a teleconference be better? Other questions to consider: Where is the market going? Are you still relevant? Is there an innovation on the horizon that will change everything for you? How do you get there from here?

Summary

If you want to stay in business, stay relevant, and stay on top of your market, you must do forecasting to look at what is changing and the direction that you need to grow. It's even more important now than in the past because of changing technology.

Happy Leading!
Jean

Don't Play Head Games

What if I do this? That person might do x thing, and then I will do y. If I can make them believe . . .

Head games backfire. When you deceive or manipulate someone into behaving a certain way, the relationship is destined to fail.

When you play head games with your teammates, you not only doom the relationship, but you set yourself up to fail as a leader. If each time you want someone to do something you must resort to manipulating or tricking that person into doing it, you waste time and create work for yourself.

Generating Ownership vs Head Games

Years ago I was approached with an opportunity that was not all that appealing to me. When I turned it down, that person quickly said that it would help Drew's Animals (my family's website). Now, perhaps it would have given me a little additional exposure, but I really did not see it helping in the way that I really needed it to. At best it was a help by association and not directly. He may have been well intentioned and believed what he said, but the mismatch between what was said and what I saw as reality brought the word manipulation to mind. I abhor head games.

When you generate ownership, you ask your team what they believe is the best way to accomplish a task. You may ask the team if the task is the next step they see in the process. You generate ownership by letting the team do something the way that they want to do it. (Was there a way to make the opportunity more appealing to me?)

Head games are about finding a way to trick a team into behaving the way you want them to behave. Head games might include lies in the form of empty promises. (The statement about it helping Drew's Animals felt empty.)

Summary

Head games are ineffective, time-wasting activities which are always found out. A real leader doesn't need head games. A real leader generates ownership through honest communication.

Happy Leading!
Jean

Should Leaders Admit Mistakes?

What if you were at war, and you started apologizing for your action against your enemy? Perhaps your country bombed an area that was really civilian and not military in nature. Perhaps it really was an accident. An apology is a good indication of how far you are willing to go. It may not be safe to admit the error. If you do, your enemy may feel free to do whatever they want because you are only willing to go so far to stop them.

Most of us are not at war.

Suppose you are on a tugboat. The captain and the crew get into a discussion about the dangerous waters and the wrong turn that was taken. They agree that there is a waterfall somewhere, but they are not sure where. The crew tells the captain that the boat needs to turn around. The captain won't admit that a wrong turn has been made because he doesn't want to look foolish.

That's really not the time to be stubborn. That's the time to own up.

Summary

Usually the situation is not as simple or as grave as either of my examples. Nevertheless, pride can keep you and your team from being successful. In most cases, it's better to admit the error and make the correction. Consider the second example. Everyone knew the captain was wrong. It wasn't the error that made him look foolish. His refusal to correct the error was the problem.

What you do in your situation ultimately has to be your decision. Make the best choice you can, but don't make it based on fear of looking foolish. Instead, make your choice based on what's the right thing to do.

Happy Leading!
Jean

Model Responsibility

While not every leader succeeds – and sometimes it's not that person's fault, only true leaders have extreme success. When folks look to you to lead, they follow your decisions – good or bad. They follow your example – good or bad. They begin to model their actions after yours when in doubt.

As a leader, it's up to you to model what it means to be responsible. Since the team is following and even copying you, the foundation you put under your team is one that you want them to be able to follow and later pass along without having to give it much thought. Small things like showing up early, acting according to procedure, and following through when you say you will set the stage for a responsible and successful team.

What if?

What about that person that doesn't follow and doesn't act responsibly? Find out why. If you are following successful practices and procedures, you'll probably discover that the person believes there is a better way. If you are unable to convince otherwise, know that eventually the un-coachable tend to wind up frustrated and move on.

Summary

When you have the option, pick your leaders. Interview each one carefully. Find those who are coachable and who you feel will be responsible.

The easiest way to grow a team of leaders is to be the leader you want them to be. Since they are looking at you, do the things you want them to do. When necessary communicate to the team why those things are important. Adopt the motto: Explain the example. Model the example. Expect the example.

Be responsible, and you'll reap those rewards!

Happy Leading!
Jean

Great Leaders Are Slow to Act

When two children come to you with a disagreement, you'll get a lot of he-said-she-said responses. Sometimes the two don't even remember everything that took place. The two stories sound similar but each is a little different. Each child tells the story such that it reflects well on him or her.

Such is the plight of all leaders.

If you have ever heard something straight from someone's mouth, but realized later that you missed a word or misunderstood, you'll know what an inconvenience that can be.

I've told at least one story that was immediately conveyed differently with me standing there to hear the new conveyance. Huge chunks of the story were left out and the message of the story changed considerably. In another case, the time frame was dropped, and that changed the meaning entirely.

Leaders must be careful not to act on a story. It could be an innocently misconstrued story. Intent and meaning could be very different from reality. Always give your team a chance to speak up before you flare up.

Summary

We all like to tell stories. Stories convey meaning and carry your point to the heart of the reader and the listener. When a story is told, there is no guarantee that it won't be misunderstood. If you are the teller, keep them positive because they will be repeated. If you have to sort out a misunderstood story, at least you won't be embarrassed by the truth of what you said. If you are the listener, remember to not repeat stories that aren't yours. Before you act on what you heard, get the facts from the source.

Happy Leading!
Jean

Not the Job of the Leader to be Liked

Years ago, I was a director for an organization. That organization had rules about membership and attendance. In order for everyone to get the most out of being a member, those rules needed to be followed. When they weren't, it hurt the whole group. It especially hurt the folks who would most likely receive referrals from those who were absent.

As a director, I tried to encourage the members to enforce the rules. This was not popular because it meant that folks who would not follow the rules would, through a process, be removed from the group. I knew that if those folks weren't removed, others would also stop following the rules, the group would weaken because the value of being there was diminished, and eventually the group could collapse.

The Job of a Leader

My job as a leader was to train, educate, guide, and evaluate the leadership teams of the groups. The job of most leaders is to do what I had to do – train, educate, guide, and evaluate. Nowhere in my job description did it say I had to be liked. Actually, worrying about being liked would have interfered with my ability to do my job. I would not have been able to say the unpopular things that needed to be said. It was, however, the unpopular things that they needed hear to encourage them to make decisions that would lead them to success.

Summary

If you are going to be a good leader, you must lead. Although it can help to be liked, real leadership is about doing the right thing, and it's not about doing the popular thing. Sometimes it's hard, but in the end it's always worth it.

Happy Leading!
Jean

Be True to Self

From time to time, I start a post or a tip, and I wind up somewhere other than where I thought I was going. Life can be that way too. It's also easy to drift. It's easy to think we are headed in one direction, and then we find ourselves in quite the opposite direction.

Companies have vision and mission statements, and perhaps we should too! We should at the very least have some idea of where we want to go in business and in life, and how we'd like to get there.

Be True to Self

I recently made a huge course correction. I decided to pause for 2 years, catch up my writing, shore up my other projects, and explore a new business venture. Instead of marching ahead in the direction I had been going and marketing those choices, I decided to put some of them on hold.

Those other ideas were all wonderful, but I'm not so sure they are as true to self as what I could be doing. They went in a great direction, but I'm not sure that they really accomplished what I needed them to accomplish in order for me to live my dreams.

Recently, I read or heard folks talking about how much more wonderful life is when you combine two things that you love, or maybe it was to combine something you love with something you are passionate about. Either way, I might have found it in my new venture with essential oils.

Stay on Course

I don't really believe the theory that if you envision it, it will come to pass. I do believe that if you stay on course, you will get further along. Hence, I have created a vision board. On that board are a handful of pictures – family and places. Below that is a list of goals and when I'd like to reach them.

When I forget the why, I look at family. When I need the what, I read the goals.

Summary

Consider where you'd like to be in 5 years. Write it down. Then, stay the course, and you'll get further along. Do that long enough, and you just might reach your dreams.

Be true to self, and create that reminder – perhaps a vision board - that helps you do that. In the end, you'll be glad you did.

Happy Leading!
Jean

Be a Giver

The Taker

Have you ever had someone ask you to help them? Then, ask you again. Each time the request took more and more of your time. Eventually, the requests may spread to helping a friend of the person you were initially helping.

As this continued, you may have found that you didn't feel like a giver. Instead, you felt used. You meant to be helpful, and you were initially. Later, you became free labor.

The Giver

You can give anytime you'd like, but you might find the most rewarding time to give is when you invest in another person. This is when you teach another person something that will make a difference in that person's life going forward. This includes both skills and life lessons.

This isn't when you give expecting a return, but when you truly teach someone or coach someone in such a way that the knowledge gained or personal growth gained has an impact.

Summary

You will meet users along the way. Sometimes, folks forget or don't understand that you were helping for a specific reason. You may find it helpful to clarify. In the end, it's much more rewarding to be a giver and invest in others than to be a taker. When a giver comes into your life, remember to look for ways to give back. You'll be glad you did, and the giver will feel appreciated!

Happy Leading!
Jean

Goal: Work on the Company

Whenever a business owner starts a company, that owner typically has to work both on and in the company until it gets off the ground. At some point, the owner will need to change hats in order to expand the business.

Some businesses do not allow this transformation – at least not easily. As a speaker, I am the product. Folks will want to hear me. Some speakers have managed to extend their company in such a way that the company brand and not so much the personal brand gets the attention, but it's a challenge.

Another example: I knew a photographer. He hired other photographers. Everyone wanted the owner. His reputation preceded him. I get that because I always want the owner too!

This is exactly how it is in leadership. When you are the leader, you still may need to be involved in production, but you also need to set aside time for professional development and planning / preparation for the direction of the company. You cannot work on both the big picture and the details at the same time. They are separate entities.

As a leader, you may eventually move up the ladder or grow your team to the point that you can spend all of your time working on the company instead of in production.

If you are the business owner, the company cannot grow if you don't. Many business coaches teach this and books have been written on the topic. The general concept is that more work gets done with more folks on your team, but someone has to lead. That someone is you. Growing your team frees up your time to do this.

Summary

One of the most important ways you can spend your time as a leader is working on the company and not in it. If you are not there yet, consider making this a critical goal. Plan activities that will take you forward financially with this in mind. Elicit the manpower that will enable you to step back.

Then, when you do find yourself in the position to spend your time working on the company and not in it, remember to pay attention to the details. You may not be doing production, but you still need to know what is going on. You cannot ever give up this responsibility.

Happy Leading!
Jean

Delegate the Load

If you know me, you will never ask me to cook for an event. Not only do I not enjoy it, but something will go wrong nearly every time.

When I'm in the kitchen, disaster often happens. Shatter proof bottles break, gas units ignite with a burst, potatoes become chard, toast becomes burnt, spaghetti sticks to the pot, and fire trucks may show up – hopefully once was enough when it comes to fire trucks. Most folks don't want to deal with the mess and my lack of reliability. Takeout is something I do well.

Why Delegating is Important

As a leader, I quickly become known for my delegating. (Tip #17 spoke of what not to delegate.) It's not that I want to get out of certain tasks – although it might be in the best interest of the team, but the team can get more done when those best suited for a task are in charge of it.

The Benefits to the Individuals and the Team of Delegating

When a team member points out something during a team meeting that needs to be done, I quickly ask, "Who needs to be the one to do that?" It's a great question because delegating the task keeps folks involved and gives them a since of accomplishment when it's done provided the right folks are on it.

When the wrong folks are on a task, it can be personally frustrating and even embarrassing to the individual(s) involved.

The Benefits to the Leader of Delegating

Delegating gives the leader time to contemplate the next step and opportunity to coordinate the details so the tasks come together as they should. Leaders will always need time to plan even if the tasks are familiar because life happens. Some could call in sick, need to leave early, etc., and leaders must take every possibility into account. The less often the task is performed, the more planning will be needed to be sure that nothing is missed.

Summary

Years ago, when I was president of a club in an organization, at the end of my term one of my teammates said it had been a privilege to serve under my leadership. She said that I had worked it like it was my job. In reality, they had worked very hard. I really did delegate a lot, but yes, I also worked it like it was my job when it came to the thought and planning before each business meeting. I had stayed on top of things.

When delegating is done correctly, no one minds because the wisdom shows in the results, and the leader is recognized for behind the scene hard work. Never be afraid to delegate. It's not bossy to ask someone or a group of folks if they would take on a task or who they feel is best person / people for the job. Instead, it shows leadership.

Happy Leading!
Jean

Rewards of Leadership

Over the years, I've spoken at free and paid events. I've spoken to large and small audiences. I've seen folks who tried to get the most out of a workshop, and those who sat in the back of an audience and chatted. You can't make folks appreciate the value in what you have to offer as a speaker. The same holds for leadership.

Make a Difference

The greatest reward you will ever receive as a leader is when you see results from the time you invest in the personal / professional development of another person. Both personal and professional growth go hand-in-hand. Often there is a personal challenge that has to be overcome in order for professional development to occur.

My biggest personal challenges over the years can be summed up with two words – dislike and fear. Dislike was often overcome by training, education, or building my skills. Fear – mostly of success – has been overcome by clearly understanding the implications of success and seeking opportunities that would provide the benefits and lifestyle that I want to live.

Probably the same or similar challenges exist in the people you lead. Your challenge is to help them beyond their struggles. When someone does not advance, it's important to recognize or find out what stands in the way. Sometimes a simple word of encouragement or direction can make all the difference.

Be Patient - Often folks must hear the same information a variety of ways before they finally get it. Others may catch on quickly, and still others never learn.

Seek the Coachable - Remember the old cliché: "You can lead a horse to water, but you can't make him drink." Look for those who not only want and need help, but are willing to let you help them.

Summary

You can't help everyone. You can make a huge difference for some. You will feel very rewarded when you do. Don't force coaching on anyone. Take it slow with those who wish it. Work on one challenge at a time.

Happy Leading!
Jean

What Will Be, Will Be: Your Team is Influenced by What They Believe

"Whatever will be, will be whether it ever is or not."

That's what my dad told me that his mom used to say – or something like that. She meant that if you believe it, for you, it's as if it has already happened. You are affected by your belief. Teams are the same way.

Teams will act on what they believe even if that belief is false. As a leader you are responsible for giving your team 20-20 vision. You need to help them see the truth in order for them to perform their tasks to the best of their abilities.

If your team is afraid every minute to take a break from the task at hand because of potential job loss, then, they won't take vacations. Yes, you may think that you get extra work done, but at what cost? Over time this is an expensive belief.

If your team believes things are better than they really are, they may be disappointed at pay raise, commission, or bonus time. If they believe things are worse than they really are, they may start job hunting or become too frustrated to continue pushing forward.

Sometimes the truth is hard to swallow, but knowing the truth allows your team to plan well. Anything short of the truth creates a venue for tired, unhappy teammates who are ill prepared for the task at hand.

Summary

Your ability to paint an honest picture of reality is important to the success of your team. They trust you to do right by them, and ultimately, it's your credibility on the line. Remember, your team is influenced by what they believe. Speak wisely, and let them believe the truth!

Happy Leading!
Jean

Leaders Follow Up

I fell in love with essential oils, and I decided to make it a part of my business. As I began to let my friends and acquaintances know, I met folks who had already tried essential oils. Several folks said they got oils via someone they knew. One lady said that she had wanted to get more oils, but she had not heard back from her contact. As time went by, she enrolled under me so she could get a deal and order herself.

In other business ventures, I have found the same to be true. Folks who were unhappy with the turnaround time of a project would come to me as both my communicating with them and my turnaround time was better. They were not left hanging.

Accessibility and follow up have gained me new clients. You might be thinking, "Jean, what does this have to do with leadership and teams?"

Although the task is the follow up, follow up is a relationship building activity. When you follow up with your team, the focus should be as much about building up the relationship as it is about getting a task completed. If not, you are missing a great opportunity.

Which is better? 1) Did you do x thing yet? Or 2) I'm following up to see how x thing is coming. Do you need any assistance, or did you have any questions? The second one is much better, of course. It shows that you care enough to offer help. The first one sounds demanding. To some, this is a huge thing.

Summary

Following up has huge rewards. It's obvious that it keeps a team on track. It can also be used to build relationships. As a leader, don't' shy away from following up. It might feel like you are harassing someone, but when done correctly, it can be both a relationship building and profitable activity.

Congratulations! You've completed all 52 tips!

Happy Leading!
Jean

www.ingramcontent.com/pod-product-compliance
Lightning Source LLC
Chambersburg PA
CBHW020207200326
41521CB00005BA/279